FLINT
FREEDOM IN THE CAGE
BOOK I

DAKIARA

COPYRIGHT

Additional copies of this book and others are available by mail.

Mind Flow Publishing & Production LLC

PO Box 48768 Cumberland, North Carolina 28331-8768

by visiting the website listed below.

Check the website for pricing.

www.mindflowpublishingproduction.com

Formatting and Cover Design by Haelah Rice Covers

Copyright © 2023 DaKiara

Mind Flow Publishing & Production LLC

ISBN PAPERBACK 978-1-951271-66-4

ISBN EBOOK 978-1-951271-67-1

1 2

Second Edition

SPECIAL THANKS

To God for giving me the strength and the words to do this project.

I am blessed by the experiences to draw from. It has not always been easy.

With each project we complete, we are that much closer to touching the world. Thank you for allowing me to live my dream.

"A slow blade penetrates the shield."
No matter how long, how hard the journey, never give up...
slow and steady.

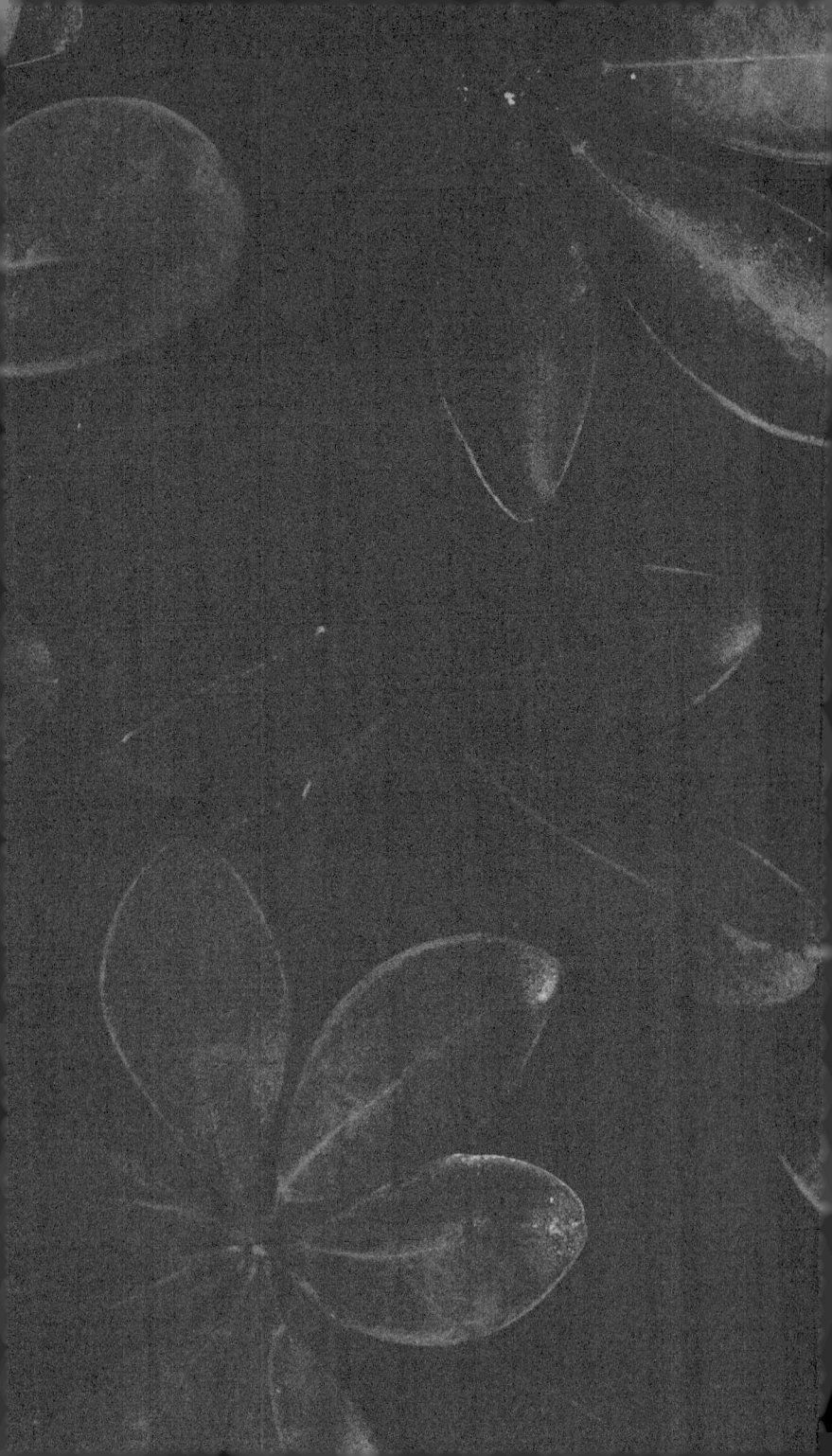

Prologue

Flint Marshall is the CEO of tech juggernaut Marshall Industries. At the age of twenty-nine, he took over his father's company, launching it straight to the top, becoming a major competitor with even Apple. He worked his butt off to prove to his father, Jacob, that he was wrong about Flint not being the right person for the job.

Jacob originally picked Hannah over Flint to succeed him in the company. Jacob minced no words when it came to his son. He felt that Flint was too fickle and flighty when it came to making major decisions.

Flint and Hannah had been competitive since the night they were born. Hannah was born first by a whole five minutes and had rubbed it in his face for twenty-seven years every time they saw each other.

Hannah and Flint both suffered from an incurable heart condition. Even at rest, their heart rates could easily escalate to well over 300 bpm. Long periods at that rate could end up resulting in a heart attack or possibly death. What was more fascinating about these two is that what should have caused them to pause or avoid strenuous activities made them crave it. They were both adrenaline junkies.—constantly challenging each other to perform life-threatening acts. For their twenty-seventh birthday, they agreed to go skydiving.

The wind reports the morning they were supposed to jump predicted that the winds were not favorable for such an expedition. For once, Flint wanted to reschedule their activity. Hannah would not hear of it.

"Little Bro, we can't reschedule our birthday. Our day was meant to celebrate life. So, do not be late. Five pm sharp. If you are late, I'm going on without you. Do not make me do that. We have never broke tradition before." Hannah had Flint wrapped around her pinky, and she knew it. He never could tell her no. This was one time he later wished he could have.

Hannah arrived at Skydive Montego ahead of her brother. She knew he might try to flake out, and she could not have been more right. While filling out the necessary forms and releases her phone rang. Without looking at it, she answered.

"Flint, I know you are calling to tell me that you are stuck in traffic, right?"

"Han, I am seriously concerned about the wind advisory. The weather isn't ideal for this type of thing. We can always do something else."

Hannah refused to listen. They always spent their birthdays together. At the age of eighteen, they made a list of things to do and places to see. The twins had never deviated from the plan before—they never had to. Hannah refused to start now.

"Flint, you can talk until you are green in the face. I know you should be pulling up in the next few minutes. We will not miss our jump window. You can't do this to me."

Before Hannah could hang up the phone, Flint was pulling up. She smiled widely, knowing that she could always depend on him.

"Hurry up before they take off without us," she yelled across the parking lot.

After parking his car, Flint walked over to the counter and asked the teenage guy working the desk, wearing a nametag that said Jeremy, about the weather.

"Hey man, is today really a good day to do this?"

The guy looked a little confused. "Every day is a great day to skydive. We did have a few cancellations due to the wind. However, we are very safe, and we only do good drops." Flint turned, looking at Jeremy with doubt, shaking his head. "This isn't a good idea."

Sweat began to bead on Flint's forehead; he started to pace back and forth across the floor. Random thoughts of what could go wrong started to flood into his mind. As if to be awakened from a hypnotic state, Flint redirected his thoughts to his sister and her rhythmic tapping of her foot as she waited for a final answer from her brother. Not wanting to disappoint her as her eyes beamed with childlike excitement, he finally nodded and said yes, he would go. Putting on their gear, the siblings talked about past birthdays and how they measured up to this one. While the minutes ticked by, Flint started to loosen up and enjoy the day with his twin sister. After Jeremy gave Flint and Hannah the once over, made sure that their gear was properly attached and secure; he directed them out to the tarmac, where the plane's engine roared. Both siblings were over-come with that familiar feeling—a burst of excite-ment, butterflies in the stomach—that hurried feeling of wanting to get the show on the road. They boarded the plane, greeted the pilot and two other employees that were already aboard, and took their seats. The pilot made a brief announcement, and the plane started to taxi down the runway for takeoff.

As the plane ascended to optimum altitude, the pilot came over the loudspeaker again.

"Remember, folks, if you hit any turbulent wind gusts, just toggle your chute cords, and it'll keep you on track. Now enjoy your jump."

This was the day he would never forget; it was the day that Flint lost a major part of himself. The wind advisory was serious. The winds were steady, which made it safe by regulation of the facility. Things were going fine from the jump, but about two minutes in, freefall was impeccable, and the twins had deployed their parachutes. Without warning, there was a sudden gust that swept them both off their trajectory. The starting altitude was only at thirty-five thousand feet, but that didn't stop Hannah from being slammed into the side of the building before careening to the unforgiving ground below. Flint released himself from the harness and fell to the ground with a thud. He tried to get up and run to his sister. She wasn't moving, but his ankle was broken. He felt it as soon as he hit the concrete. His mind was on Hannah.

"Hannah!" He yelled, knowing she couldn't hear him.

Hannah died instantly—the coroner said. Her

heart couldn't take it.—she died before the impact. Her heart simply stopped. That offered a little consolation for Flint, knowing that she didn't suffer. Why not him?

Chapter One

FLINT

TWO YEARS LATER

To burn off some steam, Flint had begun hanging out and frequenting seedy bars and clubs. He was looking for trouble. Most nights, things were cool, but occasionally he would find the very trouble he was looking for.

Tonight, Flint found himself engaged in another bar fight. This was his tenth in a matter of six months. He had been spiraling out of control for a while now. The last two years since his twin sister had passed due to complications from the skydiving accident had really taken its toll on him. The bouncer threw him out only after he sucker-punched him in the face. Flint found himself in uncharted territory. He always knew how to handle himself. Well, usually, he was fine, but recently things were not going his way. Flint was spiraling, trying to deal with the crushing weight of grief that filled his hours.

He should focus on the international juggernaut he helped build—not starting bar fights.

As Flint was about to get into his car, he felt a shove from behind. And then another.

"Hey you, yeah you. You're the one who is always starting trouble in Antonio's bar, aren't you?" Flint didn't recognize the voice.

When he turned around, he noticed it was the guy from his first bar fight a few months earlier. He wasn't alone. He had three guys with him. Without provocation, they unleashed a full-on assault on Flint. In the first few moments, Flint held his own, fighting with such intensity—he unleashed all the anger and hurt that had built up over the last few years. Flint swung like a madman, punches not connecting. He would strike five times, only landing one or two. Meanwhile, his assailants were landing theirs.

The fight seemed as if it was going on for hours, but it was only minutes. The leader hit him with a right cross to the chin. From the corner of his eye, he saw another fist coming, but he couldn't move in time. The left hook crackled against his jaw. Flint was knocked down to the ground, and he struggled to get back to his feet. As he tried standing, he felt a cold, intense pain blooming to life in his lower abdomen.

Flint was stabbed multiple times, and it took him back down to his knees. Darkness began closing in on him—he felt his life draining. His eyes closed, but he could hear conversation buzz around him.

"Well, now, you guys don't seem to be fighting fair —four to one."

"Who the hell are you? You better leave before you get some of this."

"I'm going to stay, but when I leave, he goes with me. I'm not sure what this is all about. Probably none of my business, in fact. However, I can't seem to stand by while a man gets beaten half to death. Especially when the fight isn't fair."

"This has nothing to do with you. Last chance for you to walk away, man."

"Perhaps it's you all who should walk away. When you do, this is over. Don't come for him anymore, and if you do, then you will have me to answer to."

The men looked him up and down—this guy who appeared out of nowhere and began issuing threats. The leader of the four-man crew walked over and got into this intruder's face. He began sizing him up.

"You can take him, Carmine. He's just some punk."

It was at that moment that Carmine decided to strike first. He drew back his right fist, only to be met with the stranger's left fist. Carmine could hear his fingers breaking. The look on his face told his boys to back up and walk away. Stone had not released his hand yet. Instead, he began squeezing it tighter, feeling the structure of Carmine's hand fracturing beneath his unrelenting grip. Carmine screamed out in pain. Stone released him.

"Okay, okay, dude. You broke my freaking hand. I didn't even do anything to you."

The other guys had already taken off. As Carmine looked around and saw he was alone, he too took off, struggling to find his footing at first.

Stone looked at his watch. Jade would be in soon. He gathered Flint up and tossed him over his shoulder and carried him off. Flint momentarily regained consciousness briefly before he passed back out.

Stone hoped that he wasn't making a mistake in intervening with this guy and whatever he's mixed up in. He had seen him over the last few months, passing by the gym that Stone owned. The guy would peek in, but he would keep moving. Stone knew one thing for sure, he knows the look of a man who has demons that he is fighting, but they somehow keep winning. A man who is at risk of losing it all due to reckless behavior. This man has a lot of anger built up inside. Stone thought maybe with some discipline, he could learn to channel that anger and hatred into something productive. He had watched the fight in its entirety, and the guy started out okay. Still, it got shaky quickly, simply because he wasn't focused. He instead allowed his anger to take the reins. Unfortunately, this was something Stone had seen all too often.

Stone took Flint inside the gym and sets him down on one of the cots he had set up in the back room. He grabbed some towels and applied pressure to stop the bleeding. Stone was not a professional doctor or even a cut man, but he knew enough to get by, at least until Jade came in. He was not going to let this kid die on his watch.

After Stone stopped the bleeding, he placed a thin blanket over his guest before laying down on one of the other cots in the room. He could hear his guest stirring a little, but knew he was too weak from the blood he had lost. Stone just needed him to hold on a few more hours. Stone finally dozed off just as the sun was beginning to rise.

Chapter Two

JADE

J ade prided herself on getting to the gym early every day to make sure she was ready for her clients. She never wanted them to have to wait for her to get prepped. This morning she was rushing to try and beat Stone in. She often tried, although it rarely happened. Today was no different. As she unlocked the door and was about to disarm the alarm, she realized it was already turned off. She began looking around the gym, her military training began to kick in. Jade made her way stealthily to the back, and she started calling out to see if someone was around.

"Stone, is that you? Brick? If someone is here, I suggest you call out."

She entered the backroom as Stone walked toward her. His finger pressed against his lips, signaling for her to be quiet. Jade peeked over his shoulder only to see another guy sleeping. Stone ushered her out of the room and back onto the main floor of the gym.

"Stone, what gives? What's going on? Who's the guy?"

"Keep your voice down, Jade. Long story short, he got his ass beat pretty good last night. I need you to look at him with your magical hands. Patch him up enough so I can take him to the hospital so he can get treated properly."

Stone could see the look of disbelief in Jade's eyes. She didn't understand why suddenly Stone was playing the good Samaritan role. Not that he was a bad guy—because he isn't—but he never won an award for being a humanitarian. Usually, it was because he worked with someone over in the competitions. Stone continued to go into more details about what he witnessed a few hours ago.

He explained that he had seen this kid periodically over the last few months. Stone watched him spiral from a distance and was content to stay out of it. That was until he saw the kid couldn't defend himself against the four guys. Stone could tell that the kid had some training in Jiu-Jitsu, but he could never get it going. Truthfully, a part of him saw himself in this kid. Maybe this was his shot at redemption.

Jade did as Stone ask. She always did, and he knew she would. Her current title was a personal trainer, but the unofficial one was Phoenix Risen medic. While in the military, she was a medic. She saw so much death that she couldn't take it on those levels. Jade did her years and got out and wanted to do something more with her life. Now she trains fighters, and then if the situation calls for it, stitches up the people who need it at the gym.

Jade retrieved her med bag from the locker room and some other supplies and went back into the backroom. Stone was in there waiting on her. She lifted the guy's shirt to get a look at the stab wounds. Stone did an okay job of cleaning them up and getting the blood to stop gushing out, but there was still a risk of infection, and the wounds were open and deep. Jade could see his jaw was swollen. As she ran her hand across it, checking for swelling and fever, Flint grabbed her hand. This startled Jade as she stepped back. Flint tried to zero in on this woman who was touching him, but her face was blurry.

"Am I dreaming?"

"You're at Phoenix Risen, the gym down on Apollo Street, downtown. My boss Stone brought you here. Lay still for me. You have lost a lot of blood; your jaw may be broken, and you've been stabbed multiple times. Nod your head if you understand. I need to continue evaluating your injuries. Stone wants to get you to the hospital where you can get checked out."

Flint nodded his understanding moments before he passed out again.

Jade continued working on Flint while Stone got things ready to open the gym for the day. He tells Jade that she will be running the show while he takes the kid to the hospital as soon as he comes to again.

Jade finished up her assessment and gave him a sedative so he could rest for a little without pain. Looking at her watch, she realized that her first client would be there in less than an hour. She decided to get her workout in so she would be prepared to spar if needed. Sasha, her first client of the day, arrived for her session an hour late. Jade specialized in working with women who have either been assaulted or want to keep themselves from being victims. She was good at it, not because she was a woman, but because she was passionate about women, not being victimized. She had lost a sister to an abusive husband. Jade refused to let another woman become victimized when she had the power to prevent it.

Chapter Three

FLINT

F lint awoke in a room he didn't recognize. He tried to sit up, wincing in pain. Looking down, he spots all the blood on his clothes, and the events that landed him in this predicament began to crash into him. He was a jerk to some guys in the bar, and he was being thrown out. That wasn't anything new to him these days, as he had become more and more reckless. Sitting himself up, he managed to turn around towards the door just as it was opening. Stone walked into the room, and Jade stepped back from Flint.

"Easy, buddy. My name is Joshua Stone. We need to get you to the hospital. My medic was only able to patch you up. You still need stitches and medical attention. I wanted to make sure you were okay enough to go before I tried to move you."

Flint tried to stand, but his legs were wobbly, and

he fell back down onto the bed. Stone gave him a moment and then went to help him. They left out the back door and made their way to the hospital. During the fifteen-minute drive, the guys begin to talk.

"I'm not sure why you're helping me, but thank you, man. Name's Flint, by the way."

"I know who you are, tough guy. I've seen your billboard, and I do read the paper from time to time. It seems as if you have too much time on your hands these days, well, at least from what I have seen. Why do you hate your life, or is it living in general that you hate?"

Flint drew in a deep breath, and he paid for it with a sharp stab of pain.

"I love my life; well, I don't have a death wish if that is what you are thinking."

Flint started telling Stone about Hannah and how he felt lost without her. Stone could feel the sincerity in his words. Stone could see that this guy would end up hurting himself or someone else if not diverted from the path he was on. Chasing the thrills, he shared with his sister was dangerous. Nothing would ever be the same, no matter how hard he tried. This was the connection Stone felt for him. He had lost his twin brother ten years ago, and his life had never been the same from that moment on. The one main similarity was that he was the cause of his brother's death, all because he got into a fight and his brother came to his rescue. It was two weeks before Samuel was supposed to get on the plane and fly to Iraq. Instead, he caught a bullet in his right lung. Before the ambulance could get to them, his lung collapsed. By the time the paramedics arrived, too much pressure had built up in his chest cavity, causing the second lung to collapse. He couldn't breathe.

They soon pulled into the hospital entrance. Stone got out and went to get a wheelchair as an orderly was coming out. After assisting Flint into the chair, the orderly said he would take him inside and get him checked in. Stone parked the car and went to look for Flint. The young man who took him told him they had already taken him to the back. He showed Stone the waiting room where he sat and waited for several hours. By the time Flint came hobbling out on a set of crutches, Stone had spoken with Jade twice and dozed off.

Flint hobbled over and tapped Stone's leg with one of the crutches. He was surprised to see him still sitting here, waiting on him. This guy had already done more than anyone else would have done if facing the same situation. He was sure of that.

"Hey man, umm, I guess I need to say thank you. I owe you my life right now."

"Are you good to leave? You were pretty banged up, bro?"

"They wanted me to stay for observation, but this isn't my scene. It is a little too sterile for my taste."

Flint tried to make a joke but failed at it miserably.

"Seriously, man, I'm okay to go home. I just have to take it easy and, of course, no fighting for a bit. I thought my jaw was broken. It was just popped out of the socket which caused a lot of swelling. The stab wounds are going to be just fine, thanks to you and your medic."

"Come on, let's get you back to the gym. We can regroup and go from there. I'd like to talk to you more about what happened and give you an alternative to the path you are heading down. But we will talk once you have some time to heal up. Deal?"

"Deal."

Stone went to get the car, and they drove back to the gym in silence. Flint's car was parked in a parking deck between the gym and the bar. Stone walked him over to it. They exchanged numbers and agreed to stay in contact.

The next few weeks went by in a blur for Flint. There were some small issues at work that needed his attention. He kept meaning to reach out to Stone, but he was still in so much pain, more than he would like to admit. If Hannah could see him now, she would be ashamed of him. The nerve of him going around picking fights and acting like a baby. He needed to toughen up. Flint made up his mind that he was going to call or stop by the gym real soon.

Another week went by, and Flint finally decided after work that he would go by the bar that changed his world to apologize for the troubles that he stirred up. He then walked over to Phoenix Risen and did something that he hadn't dared to do until now—walk through the door. He looked around and spotted Stone immediately. He was kind of hard not to spot. He was in the ring sparring with someone he called Brick. At that moment, Stone looked over at the door when he heard the chime. Brick took a cheap shot and caught Stone off guard.

"Good one. I'll give you that one as a freebie, but no more."

He immediately began his assault on Brick, who began staggering backward. Stone was a beast, it seems, in the ring. Watching him, it seems as if a switch clicked on. When the fight was over and he exited the ring, he was the same guy who got him to the hospital after standing watch over him. Stone walked over to him with his hand outstretched for a fist bump. His hands were still wrapped, of course.

"Hey man, good to see you not bleeding out. How

you been? Any more trouble, or you been keeping out of trouble these days?"

"Believe it not, bro, I've been just working and healing up. Sorry for it taking so long for me to get back to you. I know we still needed to talk. Between how crazy it's been at work and healing, I've had my plate full. But I'm here now. You got a sec?"

"For you, man, of course. You want some water or Gatorade or something?"

Flint shook his head no. Stone grabbed himself water from the cooler, escorted him to the office, and closed the door behind them. Within a moment, Jade knocked on the door and stuck her head in.

"Hey Stone, a guy wants to speak with you when you get a chance. Do you want me to tell him that you're busy?"

"Yeah, Jade. I may be here for a minute. Young-blood and I have some things to discuss."

Jade closed the door as she exited.

"Sit down, man, let's chat it up. We need to figure out how to use your energy for something positive. You have a lot of anger built up inside of you. It may be coupled with hurt, but there is a lot of anger. You must not let people get to you. Not only that, you need to stop looking for trouble."

Flint knew that what Stone was telling him was true. He had always been the run headfirst into, well, everything, type of person. He had no fear. Not even when it came down to facing the grim reaper himself.

"There is a support group for people who have lost a sibling or significant loved one and are having a rough time dealing with their new reality. I personally think that you could benefit from that program. I go once a month myself. I used to be there every week, but I've gotten better at handling my loss. I've learned to use the ring to let out my frustrations before they overwhelm me in unhealthy ways. The next meeting is next week if you're game."

Flint could not imagine that this guy he just saw jump into beast mode at a moment's notice needed assistance with channeling his anger. Flint agreed to attend the next meeting. *Who knows, maybe it would help him?* Stone continued to talk to him.

"Even though you got your butt whooped, you are quite talented when it comes to fighting. You exhibited some ferocity that is not easy to come by. At one point, I thought you were about to try some Jiu-Jitsu but never quite got it going."

"My mom made my sister and I take Jiu-Jitsu when we were ten. From ten to seventeen. We participated in competitions, and we both hold first-degree black belts. The parents wanted us to be able to defend ourselves," Flint laughed as he said the last part.

Stone smiled. That would help him if he decided to come aboard.

"I've thought long and hard about this, but even though the best age range to learn to be an MMA fighter is around fifteen or sixteen, you're a little away from that. But I can train you. It won't be easy; it will take lots of dedication and hard work on your part. You don't have to answer now you can take some time to think about it. Me and my guys we are a family. We work hard, and we play hard. We compete hard. If you think you want to become a part of this, I will train you myself for free. A part of me thinks I'm crazy to take this on, but I feel like you have a lot to offer and the potential to be great. Plus, if you find an outlet to release your anger, then we all win. Well, kid, that is my entire pitch. Totally you're choice if you take me up on it or not. No pressure. You are always welcome to come by and talk if you need to."

Flint was speechless for a minute. This could be his answer. After a few minutes of silence, he asked Stone where he needed to sign up at. He was all in.

"Alright, I'll introduce you to the rest of the family. You ready? Your life will change from this moment on. It's no longer just you against the world. Instead, it is the world against Phoenix Risen. Just as the name implies, we rise, despite how far we've fallen."

Stone stood up and headed for the door. When he got there, he turned and waited for Flint.

"Remember, once you cross this threshold, it's a whole new ball game. So far, you have no strikes but get three, and you're out."

Flint stood up and followed Stone through the door. That was the moment when his life changed.

Chapter Four

JADE

Jade's first client of the day showed up thirty minutes early. They had begun their preliminary warmups. Normally she doesn't take on male clients, but the money was good, and she could use it now more than ever. Jade took on about five male clients to increase her pay to help cover some newly developed expenses. Her mother was forced to stop working when she suffered her second mild heart attack. Although she fully recovered, the doctor was very insistent that she does not exert herself. He told her that her heart couldn't take it. Jade paid the bills for the house, plus medical expenses. Her mother's copay jumped up from $10.00 to $50.00 per visit. Unfortunately, she had to attend several appointments monthly. Jade didn't want her mom to worry about any of that. She simply wanted her to rest and enjoy the rest of her life.

She and Kevin began to spar. He seemed to be catching on pretty quickly. This was his third session with her. He honestly creeped her out a little, but at the end of the day, money was money.

"Come on, Kevin. That's it."

She hadn't noticed when Flint arrived.

"Keep them coming."

Her mind trailed off a bit as she wondered how Flint was doing. Stone hadn't really said too much when he got back from the hospital, except he got the treatment he needed. He also told her that she did a hell of a job of bandaging him up. The hospital staff complimented her on that. In all the years she's been at the gym, she hadn't seen Stone react that way over someone starting a commotion in the streets. Now when it came to gym family, that was something altogether different. He would go to war for any of these guys or girls. Unfortunately, his loyalty had been tested once or twice, and Jade was there to witness it. The beating he unleashed was scary in its intensity.

Jade's thoughts drifted back to the guy and hoped that he was doing well. It was right at that moment she caught a glimpse of him coming out of Stone's office. Her body was on autopilot, and she didn't see it coming when Kevin's right hook landed square on her jaw. She stumbled back, shaking her head.

"What in the...?"

Before Jade could react or Kevin could explain, a body jumped into the ring. She could tell it was a man, but he was just a blur.

"Wait, man. I didn't mean to hurt her," Kevin yelled out.

It was too late, as the man rained down several blows upon poor Kevin, one in the face and the other in the gut. Kevin doubled over and fell to the floor.

Jade couldn't believe what was happening.

Chapter Five

FLINT

F lint's eyes connected with Jade's at the same moment she saw him. A smile crossed his lips. He began to think of how he would repay her for helping him out when he was down. She saved his life. He owed her and Stone a huge debt of gratitude.

He and Stone were headed over to where one of the other guys was working out alone. Just as Stone was about to introduce him, he bolted for the ring. Out of the corner of his eye, he saw Jade get hit, and it was a hard hit. It made her stagger back a bit. Before she could adjust and react, Flint was inside the ring. He punched the guy repeatedly in the face and stomach until the guy began to double over. That didn't stop the assault, though. Nothing did until he was pulled off.

Stone grabbed him up like he was nothing and

threw him over the top rope of the ring. His facial expression was lethal, and he had no words until they were out of the ring. He shoved Flint back towards the office.

"What do you think you are doing?" Stone asked aggressively.

"I saw that dude hit Jade hard. I just reacted, man. She is a girl. Well-woman, you know I mean."

Stone didn't like what he was hearing, so he jumped in and cut Flint off.

"Bruh, do you honestly think she would be working here, as a trainer no less, if she wasn't capable of knocking most of the sleazebags on their asses that come through that door? Jade has worked hard to secure her place at this table, and she is a great girl and worthy of going toe to toe with any adversary. I will not let you take that power away from her. She isn't some defenseless damsel in distress. If she needed help, she knows what to do to get it."

Flint was pissed. Here he was trying to do the right thing, but it turned out that was not the right way to do it.

"Dude, I saw the hit. It hurt her. Whether she admits to it or not. No man should put his hands on a woman. My mom went through that with my dad. Don't get me wrong, my father was good, but he could be an asshole, especially once he got a few drinks in his system."

Flint sat down and started shaking his head. He knows he may have overreacted, but he blanked out. This had only happened one other time, and that was when his father raised his hand to his mother. It was like a switch turned on inside. When he got that mad, Hannah was always his calm to his storm.

"Ughhhh."

"The good thing for you, Flint, is that I told you before we walked out of this office that you had three chances. I'm going to take one from you because of that display, and I will explain why. Not only did you take away the power over the situation from Jade, but you put my gym in a position where there could be backlash, lawsuits just to name a few. We have to make this right. You still have two chances. Here we have rules that we abide by. Pretty simple. If you're in that ring, then you have to own that ring. No one jumps in to save you unless it's truly life or death. We don't coddle you here. We do build upon your skill level and show you how to control yourself. This isn't about killing someone, but about knowing if your life depended on it, you could. If you can abide by these rules, then we're good, man. I won't say all is forgiven, but we are good."

Flint couldn't believe how calm Stone was while

talking to him. It was a complete 360 from how he was thrown over the top rope and out of the ring. He was thankful he managed to land on his feet. That concrete floor he imagined was just as hard as it looked.

"Stone, listen, I owe you a lot. There is no other way for me to say it. Now that I know the rules, I can dig it. Something like that won't happen again. Tell me how to make it right, and I will do it."

"First, you are going to have to deal with Ja..."

His words abruptly cut off when the sound of angry footsteps approaching made them both look towards the door.

Chapter Six

JADE

J ade had never been so heated in all her life. After making sure Kevin was okay. Luckily, it was only his pride. Jade profusely apologized and assured him that nothing like that would happen again.

"You guys are crazy here. I've never been so humiliated in my life."

"Kevin, I'm not going to say you deserved that, but you know, and I know, that you took a cheap shot. The difference is that once I get into the ring with you, I'm willing to take that risk. My goal is to make you better prepared to defend yourself. He is new here, so he doesn't know all the rules, but judging how long he and Stone are in the office, he is learning them now."

"Yeah, well, I ought to sue."

Kevin felt his face and sighed.

"You know there is a way to make it right."

Jade walked off, heading toward the office. She knew what it was going to take before he even spoke it. That irritated her more than anything, having to be put in that position.

Without warning, she suddenly bursts into the office.

"I'm not sure what the hell you thought you were doing? But here, we don't do that. We don't beat up our customers or interfere with training sessions."

She paused to take a breath, and that was long enough for Stone to intervene. He grabbed Jade by the waist and gently slides her back. Since entering the room, she closed the gap between herself and Flint. Stone's experience led him to believe Flint may be in danger.

"Jade, calm down. I've already dug into him and ripped him a new one. He didn't understand our rules or our ways. I think we finally came to an understanding."

Jade backed off but still stood there seething.

"You have no idea what you have done. This man is talking about suing. I mean, I know he is blowing smoke, but what if he wasn't?"

Jade didn't close the door behind her when she barged in. Kevin saw his chance to make a nuisance of himself. He was finally going to get something he had been working on since before joining the gym and insisted that it was to be Jade who would train him. Stone didn't like it for multiple reasons. The main one was he simply didn't trust the guy. Jade was like a sister to him. The last thing he wanted was her stressed because some jerk was coming on to her. She had been through enough.

Stone stopped Kevin at the door.

"Hold on, Kev. I know your feelings are hurt. Truthfully, there was no harm done, and you know it, right man? He saw a woman being hit, so he jumped to her defense."

Kevin wasn't to be denied.

"Take it easy. There is a simple solution to this problem we seem to have in front of us. I want her."

Kevin pointed to Jade. Stone shifted his stance because he instantly became uncomfortable. Did this guy really just ask for Jade like she was an object to be simply handed off? His blood began to boil. Stone wanted nothing more than to punch the daylights out of Kevin, but that would only make things worse. This whole time Flint sat quietly, squeezing his fists together. He felt rage building up in him all over again. However, he remained calm, following Stone's lead. He was in awe that Stone's conversation resonated with him so soon. Jade was the first to speak.

"If that will make this misunderstanding go away. Name your terms quickly before I change my mind."

Kevin smiled a devilish grin. He wasn't attractive in the least bit to Jade. Kevin was a smoker, so his teeth were stained with various shades of yellow and brown. His clothes always reeked of stale cigarettes, which Jade detested.

"Don't wrinkle your nose up at me, beautiful. I just want one date. You can even pick the place if you like. It doesn't even have to be a romantic date, but a date, nonetheless. You know I've been watching you. I know you feel my eyes upon you."

"You are a manipulative son of a..." It was becoming an ever-increasing struggle for Stone to keep his composure. "The answer is no, do what you need to, man, but the answer is no."

Flint was waiting for his chance to chime in.

"Kevin, dude, why don't you just come after me. Leave her out of it. Name your price."

"You don't get it, do you? I've been trying to get close to Jade for a while now. She has been above board with me since day one. And now, I finally get what I want."

Flint and Stone both agreed that this wasn't something she should do, but Jade was headstrong and wasn't going to let this turn into something more when she could nip it in the bud. One date wouldn't kill her. She even hoped this would be the end of her having to train him. And for that, she would sacrifice herself and go on this date.

"Stone, Flint, I'm good to go on a date. This way, everyone gets what they want, and we can get back to normal. Kevin, when do you want to do this? Does next weekend sound okay?"

Kevin agreed and turned and walked out of the room. During the exchange, some other gym members came over to make sure everything was okay. This seemed to be the perfect time to introduce Flint to them all.

"Hey guys, this troublemaker is Flint. He will be joining us indefinitely. Flint, this is my little brother Brickson or Brick as we call him. I call him brother because that is what he is to me. There are a few people I hold that dear. They are all in this room. You are family now."

The guys all shook hands as they welcomed Flint to the gym officially.

"Glad to have you here, bro," Brick was the first to speak up. "Make sure you control your temper. On a side note, I do appreciate you jumping to Jade's rescue, but just know that she can kick my butt on most days."

"Alright, back to business. I think we've had enough theatrics for today." Stone told them he had some business to take care of but would be back. Flint, feeling as if he had caused enough damage, took the opportunity to head home. There was a presentation he needed to prep for in the morning.

Chapter Seven

FLINT

P hoenix Risen had pretty much become Flint's second home. The invitation to be a part of their family was just what he needed. Stone decided that he would do most of his training with him. The more he progressed, the more Brick would work with him on some wrestling techniques and takedown moves. That was his specialty. Stone was more of a kickboxer whose knowledge of Muay Thai and Capoeira was unmatched. Stone was still working on getting him to join the crew. They would all train each other to build up their house. Everyone was excited to work with Flint. Stone bragged on him nonstop. Now it was time to show and prove his worth.

Flint would arrive early at the gym, leave to work for a few hours, and then return for more training.

Being the adrenaline junkie that he was, he thrived from this.

A few days into training, he was shocked when Stone told him about a match for amateur MMA fighters.

"It's just a tournament they do every year to try and see who has the best talent coming up through the ranks. Guys from all over the state are competing. It would be a good thing for you if we can get you trained and ready in time. If not, there is always next year."

Flint was not trying to hear the next year's part.

"Tell me what I need to do. Train me. I know I am a hothead, but I'm ready. What do you say?"

Stone shook his head as if to say no.

"This would require a lot of sacrifice—hard work and determination from you. Your body is going to be put through the wringer. I don't have time to waste with someone who isn't ready to handle being torn down and rebuilt brick by brick. Do I believe you can be amazing? Hell yeah. I think you are pretty good now. You just need some refinement and the ability to control yourself, your breathing, and your mind."

Flint agreed, and they began. Stone wrote out a diet plan for Flint. It wasn't bad considering he was in amazing shape already, but Stone didn't want any garbage polluting his body. Most of the foods on the list were things he already ate, anyway. Flint was eager to get started.

Since the other day's events, Flint's mind was still unsettled about Jade and her having to go on the date to save his hide. He decided to bring it back up to Stone to see if anything would change.

In the middle of his training session, he brought it up.

"Man, is Jade really okay? I've been meaning to ask you about her."

Flint felt Stone's eyes on him, and they were not the friendly ones.

"No man, not like that. I mean, she is hella nice, but I just want to make sure she's okay. I don't want her to have to put herself in a compromising position for my screw-ups."

"Flint, you need to focus on the things that you can control. Jade isn't your problem, and what she has to deal with isn't your battle. This fight that's coming up is your focus and your only goal. I told you Jade is more than capable. She has handed out many beatings and tongue-lashings since coming to Phoenix. Her hands are amazing. Trust me, you don't want to be on the receiving end of them."

Flint laughed at the thought of her hands being a

force to reckon with. He'd felt them on his skin, and there was no way they could be forceful. Stone punched him in the shoulder with a quick jab.

"Kid, listen, clear your mind. Focus. You are worried about the wrong things. If you are wasting my time, I'm not here for it, man. I could be training others. I chose to do this for free."

Flint gets back into his fighting stance to show Stone that he was ready. They began doing some punching bag drills.

As the day's progress, Flint was getting more powerful and quicker. He was quickly exceeding Stone's expectations. It's like the more difficult the tasks he throws at him, the more he eats it up and begs for more. This kid is definitely hungry, and as long as he stayed that way, Stone would continue to feed him. *He may have a chance of winning this competition. That would be great for Phoenix Risen.* The group could use a win. It hadn't been easy pulling in clients since Brickson's last fight. He fought a great fight but ended up suffering some damage to his cerebral cortex. That rocked the family. The team didn't know how to handle it. Brickson didn't know how to handle it. He began having seizures and went through a bout of depression and severe anxiety. Now here he was, two years later and almost ready to fight again. It seems that when he went down, people lost faith in

Phoenix. Before that, thirty percent of the top fighters in the region were from this gym. Stone had trained some best.

While Stone had disappeared into his thoughts, Flint was steadily working on his bag work. Stone had to admit, watching him work was pure finesse. The raw talent that Flint possessed was something only a few people ever possessed.

"Hey man, where did you go? I was talking to you about the fight, and you zoned out on me."

Stone asked him what he wanted to know. He told him what he could expect. There would be a lot of pain and a lot of mental abuse. Flint would have to push past it all, and he would be victorious. Stone sold it so well that Flint was beginning to believe that he could win. The thought drove him even harder. He pushed himself into training. He was training so much that he was barely sleeping.

If only Hannah was here, we could be doing this together. "Sis, at least I'm not completely lost without you. It has been hard without you by my side, but I think I may have found a place where I can finally fit in. They accept me, flaws, and all. I miss you so much. Hopefully, I will have my first fight in a few months. I'm going to win that fight, and it will be my dedication to you because I know you are watching over me."

From that point on, he became more relentless

with his training. Stone never saw a more determined man, except when he was starting out.

Chapter Eight

JADE

"Hey Jade, can we spar for a bit? I know you got a client coming in, but I sure could use it. Maybe you could too."

Stone always seemed to know when she needed a friend. They sparred for about an hour. The way Jade was fighting, he knew she had some stuff going on. He eased into the conversation.

"How is your mom doing lately? I know she was going through some difficulties not that long ago."

"Yeah, it is just us now. Her sister passed last month. My mom's health is deteriorating, but she's still got them hands, though."

"Baby sis, you do know that you can always talk to me no matter what or when. I will always be available for you. We can even spar if you need to release that dragon you've got lurking inside. I've fought you before. I know what's there hovering just beneath the surface."

They both laughed. She got a few good licks in when they sparred a few years ago. Stone had this thing that you truly don't know someone until you've fought them. That was also one of his tests before he cleared any of his fighters to fight. This was no easy feat.

Feeling better after they worked out, Jade shared some of her thoughts about this date coming in another few days. Stone asked if she wanted to call it off, but she assured him she was good.

Jade wanted to make sure that Kevin didn't get any mixed signals while on this date. She was having a hard time deciding what to wear. One part of her wanted to wear gym shorts to prove a point, but she knew Kevin would find a way to make that sexual. Finally, she decided on a pair of dark blue denim jeans with a burnt orange shirt. Nothing too frilly or revealing to encourage him.

Two days later, Kevin picked Jade up from the gym at seven pm sharp. He was taking her to get something to eat at a place called Jacob's. The food was divine. It was one of her favorite establishments. You could pick your own steak, and they cooked them on the open grill.

"Jade, I know we got off to a bad start, but

truthfully, I've been attracted to you for a while. I know your rules are that you don't date anyone you train or that you work with. I'd honestly like for you to just think about it. If after today you think I'm a good guy, then take a chance with me. Otherwise, at least you will get a great meal. What do you say?"

Jade was bothered by the fact that he thought there was even a possibility for her and him.

"I'm sure you're a good guy. I'm not interested, but I agreed to the date, so I will uphold that. If we have a decent time, then that is even better, but I really don't want you to get your hopes up."

"Fair enough. I can respect that."

The two ordered their dinner and chatted. The conversation wasn't bad. Kevin was a decent guy, but just not the guy for her. He kept bringing the conversation back to him and what he has accomplished in his life. He owned two mechanic shops in the area and was about to open a third. Kevin shared that his wife left him about a year ago and took his ten-year-old daughter with her. Jade could see that it bothered him some, but he shifted the conversation and said it's her loss. He started bad-mouthing the mother of his child to a woman he barely even knew. Jade had never been so turned off by a person than she was at that very moment.

She was so glad they had reached the end of the meal. She was ready to go.

The waitress came by and asked if they wanted some dessert. Jade answered a quick no, although their lemon meringue pie was one of her favorites. It wasn't worth it to prolong this evening.

"No, thank you. He will take the check now, though."

"Of course. Be right back," the waitress left and was back in two minutes, placing the check onto Kevin's side of the table.

"What, you're not paying?"

Kevin tried to joke with Jade, and she started fumbling around as if she was looking for her purse. She shrugged her shoulders in response.

Kevin paid the check and left a decent tip. He then walked over and pulled her chair out for her to get up. When he did those simple things, he wasn't half bad. It's just when he opens his mouth. On the drive back to the gym, they made small talk. When they arrived, he got out and opened her door for her.

"So, what do you think? Can a guy get some love? A hug? Or something?"

Kevin leaned in to hug her and tried to kiss her on the lips. With one quick action, she grabbed his wrists and twisted it enough to make him turn around with her back to him. Jade crossed his arm over his chest and held him in place.

"What in the hell?"

"Are you serious right now? I gave you what you asked for. This was not a part of the deal. This ends now. If you pursue this thing with Flint anymore, I will personally go down and file a report of you assaulting me. This won't end well for you. I'm about to release your hand, nod if you understand."

Kevin nodded, and she released him. He staggered away from her, a little embarrassed.

Chapter Nine

FLINT

F lint was coming around the corner from taking the trash out when he saw what was going on with Jade and Kevin. He rushed over, but before he could intervene, Jade had the situation handled and waved him off. There was no need to end up where this all started. He backs away hesitantly. Flint makes his way back inside the gym, and within moments, Jade followed. She was alone. He could hear Kevin speed off as the door closed behind her.

"Are you alright, Jade?" he asked

"I'm fine. You have to understand that I can take care of myself. I don't need you to jump to my defense all the time. I don't need people seeing me as weak. I am not a damsel in distress."

"Okay! I get it. I'm just protective of those I care about. The way I see it is that I will always owe you a debt. You possibly saved my life. That I will never forget."

Jade raised her eyebrow at the thought of him saying he cares about her. She had done everything to deter anyone from getting too attached.

"Whether you like it or not, I owe you, and I was raised to protect others. Maybe you aren't used to it. I don't see you as weak."

"We good," Jade offers up. She turns to walk away, and Flint reaches for her hand.

"Hey, wait a minute," he immediately regretted grabbing her hand the way he did. Jade turned and instinctively punched him in the chest. "I'm sorry, I just wanted to ask you if you'd want to grab some coffee with me? Just as friends."

"Flint, I've already told you before."

"It's just coffee, I promise."

Jade finally consented to go after they got finished at the gym for the evening.

Flint walked away, smiling on the inside at the thought that she finally caved in. *Don't go getting ahead of yourself. It's just coffee.*"

Flint hadn't noticed that Stone was in the ring until that moment. "Are you ready for me yet?"

Stone motioned for him to come on.

The two began to spar—Stone lectured Flint on the need to take training seriously.

"Being talented is only part of it. You have to think and be smart about each jab or takedown. Your competition will be doing the same thing. They will fight as if their lives depended upon it. In some cases, it will. You need to fight with the same mentality only more," Stone instructed as he continued throwing punches. Flint was deflecting them and defending himself pretty well. Each day that passed by, Stone felt more confident that this guy would do some big things.

After sparring, Flint was instructed to go through his cooling down drills. Halfway through, Jade asked if he was just about ready to go before she changed her mind.

"Almost. I just need to finish this up."

Jade's last client for the day had canceled on her, so she was done. She wanted to spar with Stone, but she knew she wasn't up to it. Instead, she decided to shower and change and wait for Flint to finish up.

Before long, Flint finished up and took a quick shower, and met Jade out front. It was a nice 72 degrees out, so they decided to walk to the diner since it was only a few blocks away. The smell of freshly cut grass always did something for Flint. It reminded him of his childhood. That was one of the few things he and his father did together. They worked on the lawn. Jacob refused to hire someone to maintain it for him, that was until his health started bothering him.

"Are you alright?" Jade asked, noticing that he had left her presence for a moment.

"Yeah, my bad. Don't know why I just did that. It's been a while since I've thought about my dad."

"You are full of mystery, aren't you?"

"All you have to do is ask," Flint replied while opening the door to the diner.

As the two found a booth to sit down at, the waitress came right over with an ice-cold pitcher of water. It was so cold that the condensation rolled off the pitcher and onto the table.

"Hi folks, I'm Mary. Oh, I'm sorry. Let me grab that. What can I get you two this evening?"

Flint knew the place well; he had been coming since he joined the gym. He told the waitress he wanted a patty melt with no onions.

"Hmm, that sounds good. Let me get one too, with fries, please."

"Can I get you anything else? Something to drink, or is this water fine?"

They both asked for tea with lemon. The pair seemed to share similar tastes, Flint noticed. After Mary brought their food to the table, Flint could see Jade relaxing a little more. To break the ice, he asked her how her date went. She told him not bad. Jade looked up at him to see his response.

"The date was okay. He wasn't bad company until he kept going on and on about himself and the fact he was done so wrong by his ex. It became boring, to say the least. I truthfully shouldn't be hungry, but for some reason, I am," she stated as she looked down at the sandwich on her plate. Picking up the sandwich, she took a bite. She wasn't worried about making sure they were girly bites. This was a date where she wasn't trying to impress anyone, and it felt good.

"Well, Flint, tell me something about you that I don't know," Jade inquired sarcastically with a smirk on her face.

Flint welcomed the conversation, he told her about his childhood and family

"Life wasn't always easy. If you think I'm bad or competitive, you should have met my sister."

"You have a sister? And she's more competitive than you? I don't believe it," and she started laughing as she said it. Flint looked as if he was shocked that she would say such a thing.

Flint felt comfortable enough to tell Jade about his sister and the accident. She realized that was what was fueling him to go extra hard. He was missing a piece of himself. Her heart went out to him. That had to be hard to feel like you aren't complete. That is a love that Jade never felt as a child or even as an adult. For most of her life, she was a loner. She and her sister only started getting closer when she confided in her about her husband being abusive. Unfortunately, it was at a time when Jade couldn't help her. She was doing a tour in Kuwait. Jade thought that Mya was dramatic on the calls. Thomas never seemed controlling or abusive when they were together. She would never forget the call from her mom telling her that her sister was gone. Jade broke down and cried like she never cried before. After putting in a request through the Red Cross, they were denied due to Kuwait's tumultuous political climate. No one was granted leave until things calmed down. Their camp was taking on gunfire, and they couldn't risk a chopper full of soldiers being shot down or hijacked. Jade didn't like it at all, but this was the life she chose. This was one of the times where she hated it.

Her eyes began to fill with tears as she told Flint the story. He fought back the urge to reach for her. She was finally opening up, and he didn't want to scare her off. They were making some progress. Flint could tell she had been hurt not only by her sister's murder but by life itself. In that moment, he wished he could wipe her tears away as well as the sadness that came with them.

The pair chatted for what seemed like hours. Mary warned them when it was getting close to time to leave.

"Listen, folks, it seems as if you are enjoying yourselves, but I have a family to get home to. I'm not rushing you, but...."

"Mary, Mary, Mary, we will be happy to leave, but we were enjoying your company so much we lost track of time." Flint joked. Mary smiled, showing off her gap-filled smile.

Looking at his watch, Flint noticed that it was getting late. He had a business meeting in the morning with a huge client. This was a meeting he couldn't put off on one of his associates. The client asked for him—*personally*. It was a tech giant from Okinawa that was interested in merging with Marshall Industries. It would be a massive win if Marshall Industries remained in control. However, it would still prove to be very lucrative if it were offered at fifty-fifty. Jade broke his concentration.

"Alright, let's wrap it up so Ms. Mary can close up. Tonight wasn't so bad," she says as she stands to leave.

"Oh, you thought the day was over? It's not even midnight yet. I thought I'd keep you out long enough to see the sunrise," sensing the daggers piercing through him, he added, "Not like that... geez, give me some credit. I was talking about let's take a walk through the park. I'm sure if a mugger attacks, you will protect me."

Jade punched him in the arm.

"A regular wise guy, I see. Well, one of us has to be able to fight. I've seen the results of yours and buddy, I tell you, it's not looking too good."

"Wait, that first time didn't count. They outnumbered me terribly," seeing the disbelief in her eyes, he shook his head and led her from the restaurant. "Besides, you didn't witness the fighting, only the aftermath. How do you know I didn't damage them too?"

Holding the door for her, he smiles.

"These hands are dangerous."

"Let's go, Rocky," Jade joked with him, shadowboxing as if she was punching a punching bag.

Even though he knew she was playing around, he was always amazed. He could never deny that she possessed some major skills. Jade always seemed so effortless when she sparred. She was a natural.

"Alright, so who's waiting for you at home?" Flint inquired. He had tiptoed around the idea of asking and decided no time like the present. He soon realized he made the right choice.

"If you must know, no one really. My focus is on other things," Jade answered without hesitation.

Flint opted to head back towards the gym instead of extending their date by wandering aimlessly in the park. As much as he enjoyed her company, he didn't want to overdo it and apply too much pressure. Jade was thankful when they headed back. She was having a not so bad time, but her anxiety was starting to flare up. Jade didn't want Flint to freak out on her because she started overthinking every little thing. By the time they reached the parking lot, they were both full of smiles.

Jade spoke up first. "Thank you for pushing this. I had a good time."

"Do you have any regrets?" Flint reached for her hand, surprised that she didn't pull away.

"I told you before, this isn't what I do. I don't get involved with those I work with. I did it once while in the military, and it was a disaster. I just know I can't go through that again. Gene was kind and sweet in the beginning. Within months he turned cold and possessive. I couldn't speak to anyone without him getting annoyed or trying to fight someone. It was so bad; I was more than happy to come back home to help my mom out. So, to answer your question from a bit ago, just my mom. To be honest, that is the way I like it. Less drama and heartache, especially after what happened with my sister."

Flint, no longer being able to control himself,

pulled her close to him for a hug. The hug lasted longer than it probably should have, but he wasn't relieved until he felt her let out the breath that she probably didn't know she was holding. He was content that he could be the strength she needed. No one should carry that much pain around, although he understood. As he began to release her from his embrace, she held on. Jade raised her head just as he was moving his head, and their lips touched briefly. They both relinquished their holds and jumped back from each other. This was all new to them and was uncharted territory. Flint raised his left eyebrow and tried to search her eyes for confirmation that it was okay. Jade was searching his at the same time. The duo received the answer they were looking for as they both stepped in closer, closing the gap between them. They appeared to be compelled to try that again. Flint touched her face gently then, with quick action, brought his lips to hers.

Her lips are like satin sheets.

Jade's senses were immediately thrown out of whack; it had been so long since she was kissed. She wanted to credit this euphoria to that fact, but truth be told, Flint was an amazing kisser. Finding every sensitive spot without being overbearing. Making love to her mouth and her mind without touching beyond her face. No one had ever done that before.

The butterflies were enough to give her pause to pull back. Touching her own lips with her fingers to make sure it was real. Sensing her buyer's remorse, Flint began to apologize.

"Uh, I'm sorry...well, kind of," he said, stammering on his words. "I'm sorry if you are offended, but I'm not sorry that we kissed. I have wanted to do that since I first laid eyes on you. For that part, I cannot apologize. I know you said no in the beginning, but can you at least think about it?"

Jade turns and opens the door of her pearl white 2018 Honda Accord and slides into the driver's seat. Without words, she closed the door and drove off slowly. Flint was left watching her taillights until they were out of sight. Before he could get inside his vehicle, his phone was vibrating. He pulled it from his pocket and read the message.

"We can try it."

Flint smiled as he started his car and drove off in the direction of his place. His mind filled with thoughts. He wanted to respond to the text, but he resisted. Flint didn't want to appear too eager, although his excitement was through the roof.

Chapter Ten

JADE

Jade couldn't believe that she agreed to give things a chance with Flint. He was a nice guy and all, but it went against her original mindset. *He was just so damn sexy, though.* The first few days, they were trying to keep it hidden from Stone. They didn't know how he would react.

"I feel like I'm in the eighth grade, and we are hiding from our parents about our relationship. You aren't embarrassed by me, are you?" Flint teased with an arched eyebrow.

"No, stop that foolery. I respect the heck out of Stone, and this is new." She gestured her hands back and forth between them. "Too new. What if it doesn't work out?"

Flint wasn't in the mood to hear that. His business meeting from earlier didn't go as he had planned.

He was already sulking about that. Honestly, he was enjoying sneaking around to a degree.

"What if I just talk to Stone about it?"

"About what?" the look in Jade's eyes was borderline terrified. "Just leave it alone for now, please. It will come out soon enough."

Flint agreed, and they continued to play the game.

Jade, instead of being more relaxed at the thought of a relationship, her anxiety flared. She became more anxious and annoyed at the little things. A few of her clients noticed that she seemed tense and borderline angry.

Evie, one of her younger clients, started to acknowledge that very fact.

"Jade, what gives? You are normally this happy-go-lucky lady who I think has the world at her feet. Looking at you gives me hope that I can be strong and confident when needed. Well, until now. You have been a little crabby for the last few weeks."

Her words hit home for Jade. She hadn't believed it to be or really thought in terms that it had been weeks already since she and Flint first went and grabbed a bite to eat.

"Evie, I will be back to normal soon, I promise. There is just a lot going on these days."

Evie decided to let the conversation die off. Still,

Jade's mom was a different story when she arrived home late from a session.

As soon as she opened the door to the house, Celeste started in on her.

"Jade, come here, please. I am so glad you made it home okay. I was starting to get worried. You didn't call."

"I had a late session, Mom. Nothing to worry about."

Patting the couch cushion, she waited for Jade to sit.

"What is wrong, my love? These days seem to find you always with a frown on your face?"

Jade tried to ensure her mom that she was okay. Just a lot going on balancing work and home.

"Mom, in case you hadn't noticed, the bills are increasing. Somebody has to pay for it. That somebody is me," Jade snapped at her mom.

Celeste attempted to stand, but she wobbled and caught herself, grabbing hold of the arm of the couch.

"I know you would rather be living your best life, Jade Marie, but that is no way to speak to me. I know I'm a burden. Every day I am thankful for you and the sacrifices you've made. But if this is what taking care of me does to you..."

"Uhhh, Momma, you are fine. I don't mind doing what I do. I just don't want to hear grief about it. Nor do I want to hear about what else I should be doing," Jade interrupted her mom with an apologetic look on her face.

Celeste was a woman of many talents. She had been an up-and-coming underground fighter when she was in her early twenties, before she got pregnant with Jade. In her home country of Vietnam, on Saigon's streets, she had to fight for her life—*literally*. She entered into the fight clubs to raise money to leave Vietnam, but soon realized that she had a knack for it and grew a love for the sport. She had dreams of joining a club when she came to America, but she got pregnant by her abusive boyfriend, Shang. When he found out that she was having a girl, he wanted no part of fatherhood and providing for a family. He, too, had thoughts of the fighting world, but through a son who he could nurture and live vicariously through.

In Shang's day, he was a hardcore fighter, one of Saigon's best, in fact. His ego got the best of him, and a fight went outside of the arena. Shang was left with one eye and a hole in his skull from a gunshot that nearly killed him when it was over. He often wished it had.

Celeste became Shang's personal punching bag until she finally left. The last straw was when he punched her in her belly while she was carrying Jade.

She had enough. She packed a small bag and used her fight club money to get to America, and she put herself through nursing school. In the beginning, she would go to the gym when she could, but when she got pregnant with her second child, she knew it was no longer something she should entertain. The girls became her entire world.

Celeste hated to see her child sacrifice so much, only to end up with nothing.

"If there is a guy involved with this mood of yours, don't let them stop you from your dreams. Don't give up like your momma did."

Jade recalled her mom telling her the stories of some of her most memorable fights, and that helped to inspire Jade's own desire to join this world.

"I'm just trying to see where this is all going. I am kind of dating a guy. You'd like him. He is a fighter too, but not just a fighter if you know what I mean."

"Explain, child."

"Flint is great, he runs his own company, and although at first, he seemed a bit arrogant, once I got to know him, he is pretty awesome to be around. He is a man's man, a protector of us feeble women," Jade laughed, and Celeste did too. Jade leans over and hugs her mom, "I'm sorry. I don't mean to act crazy. He is just different. I don't want to blow it with my insecurities about men."

"Just enjoy the ride, baby. Above all else, never forget who you are and what you want. Compromise if you must, but never lose yourself. That way, you won't have the regrets I do."

Celeste's regret was that she didn't fight for what she wanted. Her girls meant the world to her, but she could have done both, and she settled.

Chapter Eleven

FLINT

During the time Flint trained, he found he had begun to calm down. He no longer needed to fight or go out looking for trouble. Stone gave him props for his dedication to increasing his knowledge of the sport and not just the physical aspects. It was hard to impress Stone, but it seemed he was doing just fine.

"Flint, give me about fifteen, and we can spar." Stone suggested heading for the back of the gym, throwing jabs into the air as he went.

"That's right, go take your vitamins, old man," Flint taunted.

"I got your old man," Stone smirked, waving him off.

Flint entered the ring to warm up and caught a glimpse of movement out of the corner of his eye. He turned to see Jade as she joined him in the ring.

Leaned into him, she whispered, "I can't see you anymore." Before quickly stepping back. Flint's face turned ghastly pale, and she grabbed his hand. He pulled away. "Let me try to explain, *please*."

Flint couldn't believe the happiness he found and held onto with all his might was in jeopardy. He tried to do everything right, no pressure, no telling Stone, no nothing. Everything that she wanted, he gave it to her. His business savvy even let him help pay some of her mom's medical expenses without her knowing. Was that it? Did she find out about that? She couldn't have.

"Jade, babe, I'm not sure why you are doing this—"

"I told you to please let me explain."

"You purposely told me here because you didn't know how I would react. By doing it here and now, you almost guarantee that I will accept it and move on quietly." He exhaled to try and catch his breath. "A part of me wants to know why, but the other parts don't. There is no logical reason. I thought we were doing good? I was happy. Weren't you?"

"You don't get it—happiness isn't all it takes. Yeah, sure, it's great and all, but there are other things I need to do and be focused on. You are a distraction. At this time, I have fallen for you, and that is not part of my plan. I'm sorry." Immediately she regretted the truth of having fallen for him. *How stupid could you be? That isn't the way to get him to back off. Uggh.*

"Why won't you give us a real shot? What do I need to do? Tell me, and I will do it," Flint realized as he looked about. His voice carried he needed to take a beat. Leaving the ring's center to retreat to a corner, he barely made the walk as his legs gave way.

He held the ropes only to feel Jade as she tried to help steady him. Flint yanked from her scalding touch.

"I'm not weak, and I'm not broken. I wish you could see that." She sighed. "Flint, it really isn't you. I want to fight, and I can't do that and be with you at the same time. I don't think you would let me fight like I need to fight. You are always trying to jump in and save me, defend me in some way. I'm not weak, and I'm not broken. This is something I must do for myself. Why can't you see that? The other side is you will be having a fight sooner or later, and you need to focus on that. I don't need to be the distraction I know I would be for you."

"You really think we are stronger alone? You could not be more wrong. I have never felt more alive than I have since we began. The last few years have been rough. Yes, I was missing something, and a part of me still is, but my life is better with you in it. Yes, you have a point. Do I want to clobber anyone who puts a hand on you? Hell yes, but in my defense, babe, we haven't talked about this before, so you're not giving me a fair opportunity to show you that I can be chill."

"We met because of your temper; we almost faced a lawsuit here at the gym because you jumped in. How do I know you won't do it again? I don't, and neither do you."

"I can argue the fact, but the truth is, if I can't show you, you will never know," he runs his hand through his hair with a long sigh. "What if we fight for it? We fight for us. Would you be willing? The winner gets what they want. You can walk away from us and be the best fighter you can be, but we do this together if I win. We don't have to choose one or the other. We are stronger together."

Jade contemplated his offer. It made her queasy, but it also made her burn.

"Done."

Chapter Twelve

JADE

"Let's do it now. No need to prolong this at all," Flint sounded off at her.

"Flint, you know this is ridiculous, don't you? This is so unnecessary."

"I'm going to give you what you want. Now prepare to fight as if your life depended on it. Truth be told, mine does."

Flint steps into his fighting stance. He throws a jab her way to provoke her to get into hers. Jade hesitates but eventually complies. Flint leans in for another jab, she strikes back. Jade taps him on his chin. Flint wasn't expecting that.

"Come on. This is what you want. Fight for it. Just know that I am fighting for us. I still believe we can do this together. I know I am happiest with you. I just need you to see it."

Jade strikes a blow to his stomach. Jade was using

all her might to land the blows. She knew she was no real match for him, but she soldiered on. Maybe, just maybe, she would get lucky.

Flint was careful not to hurt Jade, although he wanted her to feel that he was there. If this was truly what she wanted, she was going to have to earn it. He danced around in the ring a bit. With a quick movement, he closed the gap and pulled her back towards him. Her back was to his front, a part of her was turned on, but she tried to remain focused. Flint held her there for a few so she could feel the strength of his arms, and then he released her. The two went back into their fighting stances. Without warning, Jade jumped and did a perfect roundhouse kick to his chin. Flint felt it coming, and he tried to bat her foot away, but he missed it by a mere second. Her foot connected with his chin with force. He staggered back. Dropping down, he kicked his foot out to kick her foot from under her. It worked. Both crashed down on the mat. Flint quickly topped her. Pinning her down with a stronghold at first. He loosened his grip just enough for her to slide her hand first, then her whole arm up to break free of his hold. She pulled his arm around his own neck into a locking position. Flint taps the mat. He has had enough.

Catching their breath, they stand to their feet.

"Why?" Jade questions Flint, raising her voice.

"Why did you back down. You were determined, yet you allowed me to win. Did you realize at last that it takes more?"

He stands there with a bewildered look upon his face until he smirks. Shaking his head, he says.

"I love you without question. I gave you what you wanted. You won, fair and square. Do with it as you will. I won't ever have you blaming me if you don't follow your heart and dreams. For some reason, you feel as if you must sacrifice it all to have the very things you want most. You fought hard against me, so I know you feel strongly about your decision. I won't force you to choose me. I will always support you, no matter what or where it takes you."

Jade had never had a man to think so highly of her and act unselfishly. She wished she had already completed her goals and was ready for a man like him. Her mom's words held steadfastly in their place at the forefront of her mind. Pushing the thoughts from her mind to the side, she listened to her heart.

Closing the space between them, removing her gloves, throwing them to the mat, she cupped his face with her hands. She lowered his head to meet hers as her lips caressed his. Jade knew that she had to figure it out. She had to find a way to keep him in her world. She couldn't do it without him. Before she realized she was lost in his kisses, his sweaty, sloppy kisses. Flint had brought his arms to caress her back.

"Umm," Stone had walked upon them. He didn't want to startle them, but at the same time, he needed to get their attention. "Hey dude, I would ask if you're ready, but I think I have my answer already."

Jade dropped her hands from his face like a child who just got caught by their parent for messing up. Instinctively, she wiped her mouth as if she could wipe away the evidence of wrongdoing.

"Listen, you guys are grown. Just don't bring drama to the gym. Aye, Flint, I just wanted to let you know that you have your first fight. If you accept, it would be coming up pretty quickly, so training would be intense."

Flint moved to exit the ring after adjusting his trunks. He was slightly embarrassed by his half erection. Jumping down from the ring, he waited for Jade to follow. Stone continued.

"I personally think you should take the fight. It would let you gauge where you are and how well you've trained. The opponent is a kid named Diablo from the eastside. I've seen some tapes of his training. He is okay, but I think you are better. That's just my opinion. I think you have more fight in you than him. Once you decide why you are fighting and focus mentally, you are unbeatable."

Flint was smiling at what Stone was saying, but he knew not to take it lightly. He knew he had lots of work to do and so much more to learn.

"If you think I should take the fight, then I will." Flint looked over at Jade. He didn't like the expression her face displayed. "If you think I'm ready."

Jade had been quiet since Stone walked up on them. She wanted to tell Flint to wait and take another fight. She didn't think he was ready, but she kept silent. She didn't want to ruin it for him. After all, she just fought with him so that she could be free to make her own choices as well.

Chapter Thirteen

FLINT

O ver the next few weeks, Flint trained day in and out until his frustration began to eat at him. He didn't eat or sleep, and it made a grumpy Gus of him. Everyone at the gym was aggravated with his surly attitude.

"Are you going to be able to handle this dude?" Stone asked, and not for the first time. "There's no harm in saying this isn't for you."

"Nah, man, I'm good. I got this."

"Hmph," Stone groused.

"I'm just not used to it. I guess you started me off slower than I thought. I just need to develop a routine, and it will be fine. They said they have things taken care of at work, so all I have been doing is training. I don't seem to be getting anywhere, though."

"Brother, I believe you can do it, but I told you that you were going to be pushed beyond your limits."

As Stone turned to walk away, he made a slick comment under his breath, "You just need to get some, to relieve that stress. Just don't wait until it is close to the fight time. We are all going to be hurting then."

Jade was walking up as Stone finished his statement. She saw his snide grin on his face. Jade knew instantly that he had been teasing Flint. She had to admit she was worried that the pressure of it all would get to him. This was a road Flint hadn't traveled yet.

"You do know it doesn't have to be this hard, Flint. You need a routine instead of just being here day and night. It's going to take its toll on your body and your mind. You are going to burn yourself out, and even you can't fight yourself."

"Part of the reason I'm doing this is for you. I want to prove to you that I have changed and that I can be a better man than the one you bandaged up."

"For me? I never asked you to fight. Don't use me for that. You decided what you wanted to do without even consulting me when Stone brought it to you. The decision was already made. I saw it in your eyes.

Besides, you've always been just fine with me. I never saw you as broken. That is something you brought with you, and until you deal with it and let it go, it is always going to be a problem for you and for us."

Jade stopped to take a breather, searching his eyes for understanding—finding none. So many of their conversations had ended in fights as of late. The training part was great for them both, but she didn't want him to get comfortable because they handled their issues. She was surprised that she hadn't spazzed out on him already.

"Look, babe, I know you feel broken, and you still have a lot of pain from your sister. If I could help carry the burden, I would. It seems the more I tell you you're not alone, the more you act as if you are."

"You just wanted to walk away a few weeks ago yourself. Remember?"

"Dammit, Flint, but I am still here. What do you want from me?" Jade moved to her fighting stance and waited; it was inevitable. Without warning, she punches him in the chest repeatedly before he responded, only countering with a block.

"I don't want to fight you. I just want to love you and show you who I truly am. I am angry. I have issues, but I'm here fighting for you. Always fighting for you."

Jade punches him again, followed by another swing. This time, she misses. With a quick motion, Flint moves to twist her around and pulls her to him. She feels his breath on her neck. *He drives me crazy. Even when I'm supposed to be mad. Ugh.*

"I won't watch you kill yourself, training only to watch you allow someone to hurt you. Follow Stone's training plan and take a break from the gym for a day or two. Clear your head, go to work, take a shower, you stink." She freed herself from his grip, flipped him, then hopped out of the ring to storm and out of the gym.

Flint noticed that Annabelle, a gym client, watched from the doorway to the showers. After Jade had stormed off, she walked over to him to make some small talk and show her concern. In moments she was bent, putting her hands along the length of his back as if she were trying to help him stand.

"Man, that was intense. Are you okay?" Annabelle saw an opportunity to strike up a conversation with Flint. She had kept her eye on him since he joined the gym. His vision was blocked by Jade, though Annabelle knew it, which did not stop her from trying to slide in when an opportunity presented itself. This one was designed just for her.

"Yeah, we cool. Thanks for your concern. We just got some things to sort out. It's all good."

Annabelle did not like being cut short. She tried to think of something else but was coming up empty.

"Okay, well, if you ever, and I do mean *ever*, need to talk. I will be around," With pursed lips, she walked away.

Chapter Fourteen

JADE

J ade made it to her car and just sat there on the hood. She was trying her best to gather her thoughts. *Loving someone is not supposed to be this hard. Why doesn't he listen? I've never seen someone so pigheaded in my life. Hmph, he is probably saying the same thing about me right now.* She only wanted him to be safe. Jade knew he could win his match, but he could get seriously hurt like Brick, and it was taking him forever to get himself back.

Stone walked up on her slowly as she appeared oblivious to him being there. He knew better than to catch her off guard. She stayed ready to swing on most days.

"Jade, can we chat for a bit?"

"I'm not really in a talking mood, but I guess," she said as she smiled a little. "I know you're only trying to help."

"I don't have to tell you what kind of pressure my guy is under right now, do I?" Jade shook her head. Of course, he didn't. She had been down this road before herself.

"This guy is fighting for his life. When we look at him, we think he has it all together, but we know what kind of baggage he comes with. It is a part of him that he must succeed. I think he is partially trying to do this and, within a short time, to somehow make his dad and his sister proud of the man he has become. Yeah, to you and me, that is downright silly, but he is not like either of us. This was not something he was built for, but I am in awe of the fighter he is becoming. The more I throw at him, the more he takes it."

"Stone, you know I get it, but I see him doing too much, and it is pushing me away. I was already hesitant to do this with him because of you-know-who. He scarred me for life, at least life before Flint."

"I told you Lucas was damaged goods from the beginning. You just had to test the waters and got yourself a stalker who wouldn't take no for an answer. Do not get me wrong, I know there is no right or wrong when it comes to matters of the heart." Rubbing his chin, he asked, "Whatever happened to him? I wonder?"

Stone didn't seem to know that Jade knew he

escorted Lucas out of town and threatened that he would have him to deal with if he ever stepped foot back into town. Being a man, Lucas tried coming back about two months later only to run into Stone. That was probably the worst day of Lucas' life. When he was finally released from the hospital, he had several broken ribs and a broken wrist. Jade knew all too well what the man in front of her was capable of.

"You got jokes, huh?"

"All I'm saying, Jade, is ease up on him just a little. He is going to crash, hopefully not burn. Be there for him when and if he does. He is going to need you more than ever. The days leading up to a fight can be the scariest of all. One just truly never knows how the chips may fall. He is going to need you to be there. Continue guiding him as best you can, I will always do the same, and he will be just fine."

"Okay. I will keep my mouth shut and be supportive..." She trailed off as she realized they had never officially discussed or given a title to what they were doing.

Sliding down off the hood of the car, she hugged Stone.

"Thank you. As always." She dared not say he was right; he loved that crap. The omniscient Stone. But he was correct. She had to let her man be a man. It was later than she thought. "I gotta go see mom."

"Give the woman my love and tell her to have a plate ready." He winked.

"You got it." She smiled.

On her way home, Jade thought a lot about what Stone and Flint had said. It was then and there that she realized that she was in love for the first time. By the time she arrived home, she was in a better mood than she had been just an hour before. Her mom greeted her with a warm hug.

"How was your day?"

Immediately Jade knew that Stone had called her mom to give her a heads up that she wasn't in the mood to not take anything personally. She silently thanked him.

"Today was rough, Mom, but Stone helped me get my thoughts together. I told you about Flint a little the other night."

"Oh yeah, I remember you telling me about him."

Celeste saw the worried look that overtook Jade's face. She wanted what was best for her child. She always had.

"Jade?"

"Yes, Momma."

"What does your heart tell you? Listen to it carefully."

"But Momma, you told me to never settle. Never give up on what I want in life."

"Who says you have to give up one for the other? I told you don't let anyone or anything keep you from doing what you want to. You have every right to be happy."

"I realized something important today on the way home."

Celeste's eyes widened with anticipation.

"Well, are you going to spit it out?" Celeste chuckled quietly after a few awkward moments of silence.

"I'd like to invite him to dinner so you can properly meet him. And by the way, Momma, I love him. I didn't want to at first, but he wore me down."

"Did you tell him that you want to fight?" Celeste asked with a raised eyebrow. "Did you tell him you have a famous mother? Okay, well, not so famous."

"That's the hard part. He wants to fight, and so do I. We will have to find a balance between the two. I do not want him to be hurt, and he doesn't want me to be either. What if I do what he did and try and intervene, or he does it to me? It could be disastrous."

"Stop with the what-ifs. Everything going to be just fine."

Jade hugged her mom and felt better almost instantly. She went to her room to shower, and afterward, she called Flint to apologize.

"Babe, I'm here to support you, and I always will be in your corner. You want this fight and the next. I'm right here by your side."

Flint sighed through the phone.

"Oh yeah, by the way, Mom said to invite you to dinner. So, when are you coming over, before or after the fight?"

They talked some more, and Flint agreed that he would come over to formally meet Jade's mom the next evening. By the end of the conversation, they both felt better about where they both stood. For the first time in their relationship, they acknowledged their feelings. It was the first time they said the words I love you out loud to one another. They both admitted that it felt good and it felt right.

Chapter Fifteen

FLINT

As the weeks started winding down to the fight, the more nervous Flint became. He and Jade had been making real progress since they shared their feelings. When Flint met her mom, Celeste gave her approval as well. That made Flint feel more at ease. She encouraged him about the fight.

"You will win, just keep your head up, and protect your face. Always watch out for the takedowns. If my girl is working with you, you will be just fine. She learned from the best," Celeste grinned as she shuffled off to her room. "It was nice to meet you, don't stay up too late!" she called over her shoulder.

"Yes, ma'am," he called back.

Flint took the next three weeks off from work to finalize his fight plan after he had gone back for a week just to make sure the empire was still intact. He was pleased. Everything was running smoothly in his absence. He was looking at James to be a successor to him, eventually. James was his younger cousin and the closest thing to a brother he had. This was something that no one knew. Of course, he didn't feel the board would be receptive. It was okay for him to go hang out at the gym if they knew he would be still answering calls and coming in to address any issues.

Time continued dragging on, and Flint trained harder than before, but he also took breaks. His anxiety was flaring a little at times, but he remembered to keep calm. He was trying to heed Stone's as well as Jade's warnings. His mornings were filled with kickboxing and other defensive moves, and during the evenings, he worked on his jabs with the punching bag. He and Stone sparred a lot more, as well as a few other guys in the gym. Brickson had started assisting him on this last leg of his training, with some wrestling moves and takedown maneuvers.

"I've been watching you, man, you have heart—your moves are pretty good too," Brick complimented Flint.

Brick wasn't what one would call the *talkative* type, but he wanted the young guy to know he was impressed by his tenacity. Besides, everybody needed a cheerleader, *right*? Flints come-up reminded Brick of his own rise to the top. Of course, it also reminded him how it all could come crashing down like a house of cards. He wanted to make sure that did not happen to Flint.

"Thanks, man. I hear you are gearing up for a fight soon. I remember seeing you fight a few years back. You are an amazing fighter. I learned a few moves from you."

Without meaning to, Flint brought up old memories for Brick, but he smiled and continued practicing moves with Flint. Brick made progress working through his anxiety, and he did not want to dump his problems on the new guy.

Flint gave his all in his workouts. He was determined to come out the winner, with his fighting debut looming just around the corner. Jade and Celeste had invited him over for dinner later that night. Celeste was making sushi, one of Flint's favorites.

Although things between him and Jade were better, the bulk of their time had been spent at the gym working out. A few times a week, they would make time to go to their favorite diner. But there was still something missing.

Flint finished his workout and headed to the showers. As he checked the time on his watch, he was in jeopardy of running late.—good thing he had thought ahead and brought his "impress the mother gear." He stripped down, and as he reached to turn the shower on so the water could warm-up, he felt someone enter the shower room. It wasn't a big deal because the showers were basically unisex with only a partial wall to separate them.

"A dude is in here," Flint yelled out.

He wanted to make sure everyone stayed honest. Stone had told him before that there were a few incidents where people had walked in on each other. Just then, Anna poked her head around the corner.

"Oh hey, it's Flint, right? I've seen you around, but I don't think we've officially met. My name is Annabeth, but my friends call me Anna," she said as she extended her hand out for a shake. Within a moment, she pulled it back when she realized he was still in the shower. "I'm sorry, I do apologize," she said, not diverting her gaze.

"Nice to meet you, Annabeth, but I'm kind of in the middle of something. Not to be rude or anything, but I'd like to finish it if possible. I'm already running a little late."

"I guess I'd better let you get back to it then," she smiled wickedly before turning to exit the room. "I'll be seeing you around, and oh, the nice little package you have there."

Flint was baffled and borderline annoyed at what just transpired. Before Jade, he would have been flattered and possibly even exposed himself further. *How dare she say little package. If it were just a few months prior, he would have shown her just how little it was not.* Shrugging the interaction off, he continued with his shower, and his thoughts went back to Jade. He was loving the idea of loving someone. It was amazing how much he had changed in such a short time.

Later that night, when he arrived for dinner, he knocked on the door, and straight away, the door swung open as if they were trying to beat him to the punch. Jade smiled at him and opened the door all the way. She reached for his hand and guided him into the house. After a few steps, Flint tugged on her hand and made her turn slightly towards him. He found his opportunity, and he leaned in for a kiss. Jade never tired of those soft kisses that he gave her. No matter how simple they were, they remained intimate and sensual. No wonder he made her southern region flutter frequently. Jade knew if she was going to attempt to entice him, she needed to hurry. Time was running out. If anything, she believed in the old wives' tales, especially when it came to fighting. The number one rule was no sex in the few days leading to a fight. This was thought to weaken the fighters. A few fighters had blamed their lack of leg strength on their sexual appetites. Jade refused to be the cause of Flint losing a fight, much less his first-ever.

Flint made his way to the living room to wait for Jade to finish in the kitchen. Celeste shuffled through the door with a huge grin on her face.

"Come here, Flint, it's so good to see you again," she said as she extended her arms for a hug.

Flint rose to stand up as soon as he heard her coming. He knew it was important for Jade that he and Celeste hit it off. Just as quickly as she shuffled in, she shuffled out after her hug. Celeste knew tonight was an important night for Jade, and she wanted it to go off without a hitch.

"Jade," she called out.

"Yes, Momma. I am fixing your plate now. Do you want it in the kitchen or in your room?"

Celeste motioned for her to take it to her room. She half-whispered; she was going to make herself scarce so they could have some privacy. As she headed for her room, she waved to Flint.

"Have a good night, young man."

After seeing to it that her mom was settled, Jade invited Flint into the kitchen so they could eat. Her mind kept flashing that tonight had to be the night. She needed Flint to know that she was serious about their relationship.

Once their plates were made and the couple enjoyed their private dinner, Flint felt a need to tell Jade about his encounter with Annabeth. He wanted to be honest because he had an uneasy feeling about the whole experience. Something had been nagging in the back of his mind since the encounter happened.

Jade was just about to bombard him with questions about his day when Flint offered the information willingly.

"Babe, so the strangest thing happened today while at the gym."

Jade looked intently and with purpose at Flint as he talked. *This sounded interesting already.*

"You know that girl Annabeth, right? Well, while I was in the shower, she came in, and of all things, she introduced herself and insulted me at the same time."

"How so?" Flint did not like the steely look she gave him at that moment.

"She called my package little, babe. He isn't small, is the babe?" Flint looked down at himself with a smirk on his face. Jade was not amused. The only part of the convo she keyed in on was the fact that Anna was even attempting to push up on her man. Even though it was not publicized at the gym, most people knew they were an item. Anna was infamous for being quite the flirt, and she would often throw her finishing line out and see what she could hook. A part of Jade was happy that Flint did not respond in a way that would invite her to try again, but she knew Anna was not to be trusted. Jade was more determined to consummate her and Flint's relationship that very evening.

Without further thought, Jade stood from the table. She then walked around to where Flint sat. He inherently slid his chair back and was about to stand when Jade sat down on his lap and straddled him, facing him. She brought her mouth within inches from his.

Flint was taken by surprise and was unable to get out a word coherently.

As Jade felt his private parts harden against her own warmth, she kissed him with everything she had in her. Although this is not how she imagined things playing out, now seemed like the perfect time to show Flint that she was all in.

"I guess it's only logical since people are questioning your size that I investigate and get to the bottom of the problem." She teased him with her tongue as she flicked it gently back and forth across his ear.

Flint was not in the mood to be toyed with. He raised up with her still locked around him and asked her to show him where to go. Without words, she directed him to her room. It took everything in him to move quietly, to not disturb Celeste. Jade pushed open her door as Flint quietly entered, lightly pushing the door with his foot, and with one smooth action, he laid her on the bed. Jade's mind and thoughts began to race. She did not want to move too fast, but she was turned on even more than she felt the warmth intensify between her thighs. Immediately she began sliding her skirt down her well-toned legs. This simple act drove Flint into a frenzy. He released his hold on her long enough to begin stripping as well. At that moment, all caution was thrown to the wind. He did not care who heard him. All he knew was that he needed to be inside of Jade, and he had waited long enough.

While Flint was stripping down to his birthday suit, Jade did the same and excused herself to the bathroom to freshen up. By the time she returned a few moments later, Flint was laid out with anticipation. Jade eased onto the bed. But even that was taking too long for Flint. He grabbed her and pulled her onto him. Once he was sheathed inside of her, he let out a sigh. She felt it too. Jade exhaled. They had both been anticipating this day for so long that now that it was here, the emotions overtook them. With each thrust inside of her, she became more his than with the last. After what seemed an eternity, they were spent. They lay cuddling until sleep claimed them both.

The next week leading up to the fight was spent

training extra hard. Jade refused to allow things to go sideways because they could not or would not wait any longer. The entire time Jade was right there pushing him every step of the way.

Finally, the eve of the fight was upon them. All had been quiet and going well without incident. Stone was constantly impressed with how hard Flint was pushing himself in his conditioning.

Jade, being superstitious, thought things were going a little too well. When she was discussing it with her mom, Celeste assured her that all would be okay.

"Stay focused on the task at hand. Get through the first, and all others will be a piece of cake."

Jade wanted to believe her, but there was this nagging feeling in her gut she just couldn't shake. She did not know just how right she was. Later that evening, while the gang was celebrating what was to come, she received a text from an unknown number. The message was a picture of Flint in the shower. She immediately looked around the gym to see if Annabeth was there. There was no sign of her. Jade knew it was more about ruffling her feathers than anything else, and Flint had already told her what happened. She was not going to let this foolishness interrupt Flint's mindset, or hers for that matter. He needed to stay focused on his opponent and the fight.

Stone thought it better for Flint to stay the night at his place.

"Just in case you two can't seem to cool it. We can't take any chances."

Flint wanted to protest, but he knew it was not going to do any good. When Stone's mind was made up, there was no changing it. A lesson he was reminded of constantly during training.

"Come on, let's go kid, it's off to bed for you. We have greatness to achieve tomorrow. It will be here sooner than you know."

Flint was so nervous he knew he was not going to be able to sleep. Stone knew this too. As soon as they arrived at his place, he went into the kitchen to boil some water to make Flint some Sleepytime tea. This would give him the desired amount of relaxation to fade off to sleep without any lasting lagging side-effects that would potentially affect his fight.

Flint and Jade spoke briefly on the phone before Stone yelled, "Lights out, lovebirds!"

"Alright, babe, that seems to be my cue. I love you, and I will see you tomorrow."

Within moments Flint drifted off to sleep. Even in sleep, his mind would not rest. He envisioned each punch, each swing, and every takedown move as if the fight were happening right then and there.

When morning came, he was so panicked, and his

nerves were all over the place. As he sat up in bed, he reached for his phone, dialing Jade's number. To his dismay, she did not answer. Her voicemail served to soothe the beast within him, at least for the moment. When he hung up after leaving her a short and sweet message, his voicemail light was blinking. It was a message from Jade.

"Good morning, my love, yes, my love. Hopefully, that made you smile. I wanted to leave you with something to motivate you before arriving at the gym and prepping for your first of many successful fights. Know that I am so proud of you. You have done so much in such a short time. If, by chance, it does not go as planned, you are still a winner. This fight does not define you. I love you, and I will see you at the gym. No unnecessary distractions. Later, babe."

Flint did not have much time to revel in his voicemail before Stone knocked on the door.

"Hey, Bro, let's get shaking. Breakfast is on the table, the light, of course, don't want you weighed down or worst yet, puking all over the place," he said with a half-smile on his face.

Flint knew he was serious, though. He got up from the bed to shower quickly. He had already told Stone he was planning on taking a long hot shower a few hours before the fight. Stone told him it was not a good idea. He might be too relaxed. He settled for the quick one now and a thirty-minute one later. Stone agreed.

After Flint ate, well, more like drank his breakfast, and finished getting dressed, he and Stone left for the gym. He chatted Stone up the whole way.

Stone knew he was nervous, so he tried to ease his mind.

"Listen, man, this is going to be okay. You are going to go in, handle your business, and then we get to go home. Easy peasy."

Stone made it sound so simple as they got out of the truck and headed into the gym. When the guys entered, Flint caught a glimpse of Annabeth from his side view. She was moving fast, too fast for him to even bother with a second thought of her.

The match was to start in an hour. Flint had still not seen or spoken to Jade. He made another failed attempt to reach her by phone, but still no answer.

Flint tried to keep his focus on what was to come, but it was hard. *Where was she? Something must be wrong. She has never not responded to my calls. If she was not able to answer, she always called back within an hour or so.*

Stone urged him to clear his mind. Assured him that everything would be fine. In the back of his mind, he was disappointed with Jade. This was one of the reasons he did not really want the crew dating within the house. Sometimes it turns out to be bad business.

Just as Stone ushered Flint toward the ring, Jade showed up. She looked like she had been to hell and back. Although she tried to hide it, both Flint and Stone could tell something was terribly wrong.

Flint was the first to speak, "What gives, babe?"

"I'm so sorry I'm late, Flint. My momma collapsed this morning from a heart attack, and there was no time to really reach out. I sent you a voicemail hoping that would tide you over until I got here. But then that happened, and her heart stopped, and things got—chaotic. I'm sorry," Jade sobbed.

"Go be with her. I will be fine. I promise."

"No, she is stable, and she told me to be here with you. She said you would need me more, and when it is all over, we can both go and sit with her if need be."

Just then, over the loudspeaker, the announcer announced the fight.

There was something surreal about the announcer saying his name, and with that, it all became real.

Stone walked to the door and waited for Flint to follow. They blew through the double fire doors, which slammed behind as they entered the gym. Although Flint trained in this gym day in and day out, something was different as he walked to the ring. Flint smiled to himself. He climbed up the ring and through the ropes that Stone was held open for him. He looked over to see that Jade had made her way to an awaiting chair on the front row.

Flint looked over at his opponent, and he saw darkness reflected in his eyes. Stone had told him that this guy was going to be coming to fight. He wanted to win just as much as Flint, perhaps more.

The referee motioned for the two fighters to come to the center of the ring. He wanted them to touch gloves to show good sportsmanship. The ref went over the rules, and they both acknowledged their understanding.

"Good," the ref said. "I want a good clean fight tonight, where everybody goes home in one piece. Got it?"

"Yeah."

"Got it."

What happened next was mostly a blur to Flint. He remembered going back to his corner, looking over at Jade—she smiled.

His opponent, as soon as the bell rang to start the round, pounced on him. Before Flint realized what was transpiring, Diablo was wrapped around him and adding pressure to pull him down. Down he went with a thud. Trying to gather his thoughts, he finally was able to free himself. Not an easy task with this guy and trying to make sure he did not submit.

Slowly standing, holding onto the rope for extra balance, Flint began his attack. He threw punches, a few kicks, but nothing phased this monster.

Flint was pinned against the ropes. *This guy will not let up.*

Ding, Ding

Saved by the bell and not all too soon. The blows and the powerful punches he took in this first round had already begun to wear on his body.

In the corner, Stone began to second guess himself about thinking the kid was ready. "Hey kid, maybe we should just call this one. We can get you ready for another one when you are really ready."

Hearing Stone say that he did not think Flint was ready hurt, but it also served to snap him into reality. He was being dominated by some joker. *Get it together, Flint. You can do this.*

If Stone felt this way, he could only imagine what Jade thought. He would show them. He would show them all exactly what he was made of.

Flint stood ready to go when the second bell rang. Diablo, didn't have time to react. This time it was Flint who began a full-on assault and would not let up. Within seconds he had securely jumped onto his back and tucked his heels into his inner thighs, while his arms were like vipers around his chest. In this move, he had managed to get his opponent's arms stretched out above his head. The position was extremely hard to counter once set. Flint had struggled during the first round, so he needed this to stick. The ref began looking for the submission, and about thirty seconds later, he received it. Flint relinquished his hold and staggered a little toward the rope.

He had done it.

Stone was on him with congratulations, but it was her voice that he focused on. Jade called his name.

"So how does it feel, man?" Stone pulled his attention back from the cheers.

"I'm tired," Flint managed. He was more than ready to go home and figure out what was next. Jade had made her way to him, but just as soon as she did, her telephone rang.

In her distracted state, she answered. He watched as her smile turned and her eyes filled with tears. She dropped to the mat, and as hard as Flint tried to reach her, he was too late.

His mind raced. What was happening? How could his world crumble and soar in seconds? How could a happy time for him spin out into immediate tragedy? How would they move on from this? Would they be able to?

EPILOGUE

Jade's mother was gone, but with tragedy came hope. So much had changed. Eight months after Flint's epic fight, they welcomed a baby girl—Hannah Celeste—named after Jade's mom and Flint's sister. Baby Hannah came into the world kicking and screaming, and everyone instantly knew she would be a fighter. The struggles that most preemies must push through, she had defeated, able to come home in just weeks.

The whole crew was all in attendance for her arrival, having dropped everything at the incoming text. Stone, of course, arrived first and paced the floor as if he was the grandfather. In a way, he was, and when the couple presented her, he was the one in tears.

No one had ever seen this side of Stone before. Flint and Jade had agreed early that they wanted Stone to be their child's godfather. They even gave him a hat to commemorate the day. Flint had wanted to propose, but he did not want it to be cliché. Then the timing never seemed to be right.

After the baby, Jade began training again, and Flint was determined to be with her every step of the way, just as she was for him. He took on the daddy duties, so Jade could focus on her dreams.

This is what Jade had fought so hard for. She stood in her corner, ready. Determined, faithful.

The bell rang, and with a glance to Flint and Stone, *her family*—she started her assault. The match went on for three rounds. Her opponent was good, but not good enough. Jade was able to repeatedly knock her down, and finally, using a takedown move, wrapping up her legs in the middle of the mat so she could not grab hold of the rope. The ref began to count down, and Jade found Flint in the crowd. He was grinning from ear to ear.

The fight was not easy, and Jade still did not believe she won until the official held up her hand as they stood in the middle of the ring.

"The winner of this three-round bout, by submission, is Jade," The official leaned over and whispered in her ear that someone else wanted to make an announcement. Jade nodded.

A commotion came from behind her, and as she

turned, she watched Flint climb through the ropes with a fast approach.

Taking the mic from the referee, Flint ensured he was center stage. He waited a moment until Stone was there beside him, holding Hannah, grinning wildly.

"Babe, I am so proud of you. This is where you have wanted to be since I first laid eyes on you. Over this last year, you have sacrificed so much for Hannah and me. We can never repay you. You have shown me what determination means, as well as you have made me a better man. I will be forever grateful that you helped channel the anger that had begun eating me up inside. Still, you saw the good in me," Flint dropped down to one knee before continuing. "In front of all these people who are here for you, I need to ask you something, baby. I know what I want the answer to be, but I need you to say it. Jade, will you marry me?"

Jade fumbled to remove her gloves. She bent down, grabbed his face, and kissed him feverishly. It took a moment to realize where she was—though the eruption of hoots and hollers did help. She pulled back with a smile and a short chuckle.

Flint's eyes searched her own. He had asked her a very important question.

"Yes, my love. I will marry you. I've won it—all of it." Her hand trembled as Flint took the ring from Stone, slipping it to her finger. "Now I am complete."

The End

DaKIARA

Although DaKiara is still considered new to the publishing world, she has hit the ground running full speed ahead. In her first year, she independently published her first work. Soon after, she decided to form Mind Flow Publishing LLC, a small publishing house, to work with other authors. DaKiara has recently earned a spot on the Amazon International Bestsellers List. She has become a frequent flyer on the Amazon US Bestsellers List. Each time for her feels as if it is the first all over again. Her works are spread across genres such as Poetry, Inspirational, Urban Fiction, Paranormal, Contemporary Romance, Suspense & Thriller, and Christian Fiction.

In addition to having books available in paperback, and eBook formats, DaKiara has an evergrowing catalog on Amazon's newest platform, Vella. Some of those titles are Inn Too Deep, Split Decision, and Finding Kate. These have been some of her more popular projects. All are completed and will be moving to eBook and paperback in 2023.

DaKiara's love for writing started when she was

about twelve, writing poetry and writing speeches for various oratorical contests. Inspiration for her craft is pulled from her own life experiences, as well as others. She has been featured on several podcasts, as well as Up and Coming Authors Newsletters. When she is not writing, she loves to design shadowboxes and create personalized greeting cards.

Thank You for Reading....

facebook.com/carlette.thompsonwhitlock

twitter.com/DakiaraP

instagram.com/iamthelyte

tiktok.com/@iamdakiara

amazon.com/stores/author/B07D6GMLPK

linkedin.com/in/carlette-whitlock-889937179

bookbub.com/authors/dakiara

Also By DaKiara

<u>The Mary B Chronicles</u>

<u>For Her Love</u>

Standalone Short Stories

<u>Charisma's Homecoming</u>

<u>Dreams Do Come True</u>

<u>A Chance at Love</u>

Young Adult

<u>Royalty</u>

Occult & Horror

<u>To Be Chosen</u>

Inspirational

<u>Journey to Living</u>

Poetry

UPCOMING PROJECTS BY DAKIARA

- Secrets Uncovered Series
- Sleepless Nights (1)
- Dark Truths (2)
- Redeeming Justice (3)
- Sins of the Past (4)
- Balance of Power (5)
- For Her Love 2
- Dragon Slayer
- The Birthday Wish
- Inn Too Deep
- Sophie's Pack
- Split Decision
- Finding Kate

All titles will be available on Vella. All titles will be in eBook and paperback formats once completed.